# Easy Password

I0015997

| Site | Username | Password |
|------|----------|----------|
|      |          |          |
|      |          |          |
|      |          |          |
|      |          |          |
|      |          |          |
|      |          |          |
|      |          |          |
|      |          |          |
|      |          |          |
|      |          |          |
|      |          |          |
|      |          |          |
|      |          |          |
|      |          |          |

# Easy Password Tracker

| Site | Username | Password |
|---|---|---|
|  |  |  |
|  |  |  |
|  |  |  |
|  |  |  |
|  |  |  |
|  |  |  |
|  |  |  |
|  |  |  |
|  |  |  |
|  |  |  |
|  |  |  |
|  |  |  |
|  |  |  |
|  |  |  |

# Easy Password Tracker

| Site | Username | Password |
|------|----------|----------|
|      |          |          |
|      |          |          |
|      |          |          |
|      |          |          |
|      |          |          |
|      |          |          |
|      |          |          |
|      |          |          |
|      |          |          |
|      |          |          |
|      |          |          |
|      |          |          |
|      |          |          |
|      |          |          |

# Easy Password Tracker

| Site | Username | Password |
|------|----------|----------|
|  |  |  |
|  |  |  |
|  |  |  |
|  |  |  |
|  |  |  |
|  |  |  |
|  |  |  |
|  |  |  |
|  |  |  |
|  |  |  |
|  |  |  |
|  |  |  |
|  |  |  |

# Easy Password Tracker

| Site | Username | Password |
|------|----------|----------|
|      |          |          |
|      |          |          |
|      |          |          |
|      |          |          |
|      |          |          |
|      |          |          |
|      |          |          |
|      |          |          |
|      |          |          |
|      |          |          |
|      |          |          |
|      |          |          |
|      |          |          |
|      |          |          |

# Easy Password Tracker

| Site | Username | Password |
|------|----------|----------|
|      |          |          |
|      |          |          |
|      |          |          |
|      |          |          |
|      |          |          |
|      |          |          |
|      |          |          |
|      |          |          |
|      |          |          |
|      |          |          |
|      |          |          |
|      |          |          |
|      |          |          |

# Easy Password Tracker

| Site | Username | Password |
|---|---|---|
| | | |
| | | |
| | | |
| | | |
| | | |
| | | |
| | | |
| | | |
| | | |
| | | |
| | | |
| | | |
| | | |
| | | |

# Easy Password Tracker

| Site | Username | Password |
|------|----------|----------|
|      |          |          |
|      |          |          |
|      |          |          |
|      |          |          |
|      |          |          |
|      |          |          |
|      |          |          |
|      |          |          |
|      |          |          |
|      |          |          |
|      |          |          |
|      |          |          |
|      |          |          |

# Easy Password Tracker

| Site | Username | Password |
|------|----------|----------|
|      |          |          |
|      |          |          |
|      |          |          |
|      |          |          |
|      |          |          |
|      |          |          |
|      |          |          |
|      |          |          |
|      |          |          |
|      |          |          |
|      |          |          |
|      |          |          |
|      |          |          |
|      |          |          |

# Easy Password Tracker

| Site | Username | Password |
|------|----------|----------|
|      |          |          |
|      |          |          |
|      |          |          |
|      |          |          |
|      |          |          |
|      |          |          |
|      |          |          |
|      |          |          |
|      |          |          |
|      |          |          |
|      |          |          |
|      |          |          |
|      |          |          |

# Easy Password Tracker

| Site | Username | Password |
|------|----------|----------|
|      |          |          |
|      |          |          |
|      |          |          |
|      |          |          |
|      |          |          |
|      |          |          |
|      |          |          |
|      |          |          |
|      |          |          |
|      |          |          |
|      |          |          |
|      |          |          |
|      |          |          |
|      |          |          |

# Easy Password Tracker

| Site | Username | Password |
|---|---|---|
| | | |
| | | |
| | | |
| | | |
| | | |
| | | |
| | | |
| | | |
| | | |
| | | |
| | | |
| | | |
| | | |

# Easy Password Tracker

| Site | Username | Password |
|------|----------|----------|
|      |          |          |
|      |          |          |
|      |          |          |
|      |          |          |
|      |          |          |
|      |          |          |
|      |          |          |
|      |          |          |
|      |          |          |
|      |          |          |
|      |          |          |
|      |          |          |
|      |          |          |
|      |          |          |

# Easy Password Tracker

| Site | Username | Password |
| --- | --- | --- |
| | | |
| | | |
| | | |
| | | |
| | | |
| | | |
| | | |
| | | |
| | | |
| | | |
| | | |
| | | |
| | | |

# Easy Password Tracker

| Site | Username | Password |
|------|----------|----------|
|      |          |          |
|      |          |          |
|      |          |          |
|      |          |          |
|      |          |          |
|      |          |          |
|      |          |          |
|      |          |          |
|      |          |          |
|      |          |          |
|      |          |          |
|      |          |          |
|      |          |          |
|      |          |          |

# Easy Password Tracker

| Site | Username | Password |
|------|----------|----------|
|      |          |          |
|      |          |          |
|      |          |          |
|      |          |          |
|      |          |          |
|      |          |          |
|      |          |          |
|      |          |          |
|      |          |          |
|      |          |          |
|      |          |          |
|      |          |          |
|      |          |          |
|      |          |          |

# Easy Password Tracker

| Site | Username | Password |
|------|----------|----------|
|      |          |          |
|      |          |          |
|      |          |          |
|      |          |          |
|      |          |          |
|      |          |          |
|      |          |          |
|      |          |          |
|      |          |          |
|      |          |          |
|      |          |          |
|      |          |          |
|      |          |          |
|      |          |          |

# Easy Password Tracker

| Site | Username | Password |
|------|----------|----------|
|      |          |          |
|      |          |          |
|      |          |          |
|      |          |          |
|      |          |          |
|      |          |          |
|      |          |          |
|      |          |          |
|      |          |          |
|      |          |          |
|      |          |          |
|      |          |          |
|      |          |          |

# Easy Password Tracker

| Site | Username | Password |
|------|----------|----------|
|      |          |          |
|      |          |          |
|      |          |          |
|      |          |          |
|      |          |          |
|      |          |          |
|      |          |          |
|      |          |          |
|      |          |          |
|      |          |          |
|      |          |          |
|      |          |          |
|      |          |          |
|      |          |          |

# Easy Password Tracker

| Site | Username | Password |
|------|----------|----------|
|      |          |          |
|      |          |          |
|      |          |          |
|      |          |          |
|      |          |          |
|      |          |          |
|      |          |          |
|      |          |          |
|      |          |          |
|      |          |          |
|      |          |          |
|      |          |          |
|      |          |          |
|      |          |          |

# Easy Password Tracker

| Site | Username | Password |
|------|----------|----------|
|      |          |          |
|      |          |          |
|      |          |          |
|      |          |          |
|      |          |          |
|      |          |          |
|      |          |          |
|      |          |          |
|      |          |          |
|      |          |          |
|      |          |          |
|      |          |          |
|      |          |          |
|      |          |          |

# Easy Password Tracker

| Site | Username | Password |
|---|---|---|
|  |  |  |
|  |  |  |
|  |  |  |
|  |  |  |
|  |  |  |
|  |  |  |
|  |  |  |
|  |  |  |
|  |  |  |
|  |  |  |
|  |  |  |
|  |  |  |
|  |  |  |
|  |  |  |

# Easy Password Tracker

| Site | Username | Password |
|------|----------|----------|
|      |          |          |
|      |          |          |
|      |          |          |
|      |          |          |
|      |          |          |
|      |          |          |
|      |          |          |
|      |          |          |
|      |          |          |
|      |          |          |
|      |          |          |
|      |          |          |
|      |          |          |
|      |          |          |

# Easy Password Tracker

| Site | Username | Password |
|------|----------|----------|
|      |          |          |
|      |          |          |
|      |          |          |
|      |          |          |
|      |          |          |
|      |          |          |
|      |          |          |
|      |          |          |
|      |          |          |
|      |          |          |
|      |          |          |
|      |          |          |
|      |          |          |

# Easy Password Tracker

| Site | Username | Password |
|------|----------|----------|
|      |          |          |
|      |          |          |
|      |          |          |
|      |          |          |
|      |          |          |
|      |          |          |
|      |          |          |
|      |          |          |
|      |          |          |
|      |          |          |
|      |          |          |
|      |          |          |
|      |          |          |
|      |          |          |

# Easy Password Tracker

| Site | Username | Password |
|------|----------|----------|
|      |          |          |
|      |          |          |
|      |          |          |
|      |          |          |
|      |          |          |
|      |          |          |
|      |          |          |
|      |          |          |
|      |          |          |
|      |          |          |
|      |          |          |
|      |          |          |
|      |          |          |
|      |          |          |

# Easy Password Tracker

| Site | Username | Password |
|------|----------|----------|
|      |          |          |
|      |          |          |
|      |          |          |
|      |          |          |
|      |          |          |
|      |          |          |
|      |          |          |
|      |          |          |
|      |          |          |
|      |          |          |
|      |          |          |
|      |          |          |
|      |          |          |
|      |          |          |

# Easy Password Tracker

| Site | Username | Password |
|---|---|---|
|  |  |  |
|  |  |  |
|  |  |  |
|  |  |  |
|  |  |  |
|  |  |  |
|  |  |  |
|  |  |  |
|  |  |  |
|  |  |  |
|  |  |  |
|  |  |  |
|  |  |  |
|  |  |  |

# Easy Password Tracker

| Site | Username | Password |
|------|----------|----------|
|      |          |          |
|      |          |          |
|      |          |          |
|      |          |          |
|      |          |          |
|      |          |          |
|      |          |          |
|      |          |          |
|      |          |          |
|      |          |          |
|      |          |          |
|      |          |          |
|      |          |          |
|      |          |          |

# Easy Password Tracker

| Site | Username | Password |
|------|----------|----------|
|      |          |          |
|      |          |          |
|      |          |          |
|      |          |          |
|      |          |          |
|      |          |          |
|      |          |          |
|      |          |          |
|      |          |          |
|      |          |          |
|      |          |          |
|      |          |          |
|      |          |          |
|      |          |          |

# Easy Password Tracker

| Site | Username | Password |
|------|----------|----------|
|      |          |          |
|      |          |          |
|      |          |          |
|      |          |          |
|      |          |          |
|      |          |          |
|      |          |          |
|      |          |          |
|      |          |          |
|      |          |          |
|      |          |          |
|      |          |          |
|      |          |          |
|      |          |          |

# Easy Password Tracker

| Site | Username | Password |
| --- | --- | --- |
|  |  |  |
|  |  |  |
|  |  |  |
|  |  |  |
|  |  |  |
|  |  |  |
|  |  |  |
|  |  |  |
|  |  |  |
|  |  |  |
|  |  |  |
|  |  |  |
|  |  |  |
|  |  |  |

# Easy Password Tracker

| Site | Username | Password |
|---|---|---|
| | | |
| | | |
| | | |
| | | |
| | | |
| | | |
| | | |
| | | |
| | | |
| | | |
| | | |
| | | |
| | | |
| | | |

# Easy Password Tracker

| Site | Username | Password |
| --- | --- | --- |
| | | |
| | | |
| | | |
| | | |
| | | |
| | | |
| | | |
| | | |
| | | |
| | | |
| | | |
| | | |
| | | |
| | | |

# Easy Password Tracker

| Site | Username | Password |
|---|---|---|
|  |  |  |
|  |  |  |
|  |  |  |
|  |  |  |
|  |  |  |
|  |  |  |
|  |  |  |
|  |  |  |
|  |  |  |
|  |  |  |
|  |  |  |
|  |  |  |
|  |  |  |
|  |  |  |

# Easy Password Tracker

| Site | Username | Password |
|------|----------|----------|
|      |          |          |
|      |          |          |
|      |          |          |
|      |          |          |
|      |          |          |
|      |          |          |
|      |          |          |
|      |          |          |
|      |          |          |
|      |          |          |
|      |          |          |
|      |          |          |
|      |          |          |
|      |          |          |

# Easy Password Tracker

| Site | Username | Password |
|------|----------|----------|
|      |          |          |
|      |          |          |
|      |          |          |
|      |          |          |
|      |          |          |
|      |          |          |
|      |          |          |
|      |          |          |
|      |          |          |
|      |          |          |
|      |          |          |
|      |          |          |
|      |          |          |
|      |          |          |

# Easy Password Tracker

| Site | Username | Password |
|------|----------|----------|
|      |          |          |
|      |          |          |
|      |          |          |
|      |          |          |
|      |          |          |
|      |          |          |
|      |          |          |
|      |          |          |
|      |          |          |
|      |          |          |
|      |          |          |
|      |          |          |
|      |          |          |
|      |          |          |

# Easy Password Tracker

| Site | Username | Password |
|------|----------|----------|
|      |          |          |
|      |          |          |
|      |          |          |
|      |          |          |
|      |          |          |
|      |          |          |
|      |          |          |
|      |          |          |
|      |          |          |
|      |          |          |
|      |          |          |
|      |          |          |
|      |          |          |
|      |          |          |

# Easy Password Tracker

| Site | Username | Password |
| --- | --- | --- |
| | | |
| | | |
| | | |
| | | |
| | | |
| | | |
| | | |
| | | |
| | | |
| | | |
| | | |
| | | |
| | | |
| | | |

# Easy Password Tracker

| Site | Username | Password |
|------|----------|----------|
|      |          |          |
|      |          |          |
|      |          |          |
|      |          |          |
|      |          |          |
|      |          |          |
|      |          |          |
|      |          |          |
|      |          |          |
|      |          |          |
|      |          |          |
|      |          |          |
|      |          |          |

# Easy Password Tracker

| Site | Username | Password |
|---|---|---|
|  |  |  |
|  |  |  |
|  |  |  |
|  |  |  |
|  |  |  |
|  |  |  |
|  |  |  |
|  |  |  |
|  |  |  |
|  |  |  |
|  |  |  |
|  |  |  |
|  |  |  |
|  |  |  |

# Easy Password Tracker

| Site | Username | Password |
|------|----------|----------|
|      |          |          |
|      |          |          |
|      |          |          |
|      |          |          |
|      |          |          |
|      |          |          |
|      |          |          |
|      |          |          |
|      |          |          |
|      |          |          |
|      |          |          |
|      |          |          |
|      |          |          |
|      |          |          |

# Easy Password Tracker

| Site | Username | Password |
|---|---|---|
| | | |
| | | |
| | | |
| | | |
| | | |
| | | |
| | | |
| | | |
| | | |
| | | |
| | | |
| | | |
| | | |

# Easy Password Tracker

| Site | Username | Password |
|------|----------|----------|
|      |          |          |
|      |          |          |
|      |          |          |
|      |          |          |
|      |          |          |
|      |          |          |
|      |          |          |
|      |          |          |
|      |          |          |
|      |          |          |
|      |          |          |
|      |          |          |
|      |          |          |
|      |          |          |

# Easy Password Tracker

| Site | Username | Password |
| --- | --- | --- |
|  |  |  |
|  |  |  |
|  |  |  |
|  |  |  |
|  |  |  |
|  |  |  |
|  |  |  |
|  |  |  |
|  |  |  |
|  |  |  |
|  |  |  |
|  |  |  |
|  |  |  |
|  |  |  |

# Easy Password Tracker

| Site | Username | Password |
|------|----------|----------|
|      |          |          |
|      |          |          |
|      |          |          |
|      |          |          |
|      |          |          |
|      |          |          |
|      |          |          |
|      |          |          |
|      |          |          |
|      |          |          |
|      |          |          |
|      |          |          |
|      |          |          |
|      |          |          |

# Easy Password Tracker

| Site | Username | Password |
|------|----------|----------|
|      |          |          |
|      |          |          |
|      |          |          |
|      |          |          |
|      |          |          |
|      |          |          |
|      |          |          |
|      |          |          |
|      |          |          |
|      |          |          |
|      |          |          |
|      |          |          |
|      |          |          |

# Easy Password Tracker

| Site | Username | Password |
|---|---|---|
|  |  |  |
|  |  |  |
|  |  |  |
|  |  |  |
|  |  |  |
|  |  |  |
|  |  |  |
|  |  |  |
|  |  |  |
|  |  |  |
|  |  |  |
|  |  |  |
|  |  |  |
|  |  |  |

# Easy Password Tracker

| Site | Username | Password |
|---|---|---|
| | | |
| | | |
| | | |
| | | |
| | | |
| | | |
| | | |
| | | |
| | | |
| | | |
| | | |
| | | |
| | | |

# Easy Password Tracker

| Site | Username | Password |
|------|----------|----------|
|      |          |          |
|      |          |          |
|      |          |          |
|      |          |          |
|      |          |          |
|      |          |          |
|      |          |          |
|      |          |          |
|      |          |          |
|      |          |          |
|      |          |          |
|      |          |          |
|      |          |          |
|      |          |          |

# Easy Password Tracker

| Site | Username | Password |
|------|----------|----------|
|  |  |  |
|  |  |  |
|  |  |  |
|  |  |  |
|  |  |  |
|  |  |  |
|  |  |  |
|  |  |  |
|  |  |  |
|  |  |  |
|  |  |  |
|  |  |  |
|  |  |  |
|  |  |  |